# AN ANXIETY BOOK FOR TEENS

## AN EASY TO READ A-Z ANXIETY BOOK FOR TEENAGERS
## (WITH TIPS & ACTIVITIES)

*Ged Jenkins-Omar*

First published 2021 by Oliver Summer Publishing.
ISBN: 978-1-80049-539-5
Copyright © Gerard Jenkins-Omar

Authored by Ged Jenkins-Omar

# Table of Content

# Foreword

## By Danielle Jenkins-Omar

For the last 10 years, I have worked with young people within an educational setting. I have found that when young people are struggling with their mental health, it can often take an extremely long time for referrals to be processed and for individuals to receive the right support.

Despite the amazing work carried out by young people's mental health services, they are often under-resourced and overwhelmed with need. As a result, it can take a young person as long as 8 months to a year to receive the specialist support that they require. This wait can have an extremely negative impact on young people's wellbeing and academic achievements.

Within my profession, I have found that teenagers struggling with their mental health also struggle to talk about their feelings. However, deep down, they are crying out for help and support. It is my belief that this book can help in some way to educate, assist, and guide those who may be struggling.

This book can provide teenagers with hope, reassurance and comfort and provide positive self-help strategies that

1

can be used daily. I believe this book is not only suitable for teenagers but also for professionals working with young people and for parents too.

With an everchanging society, poor mental health is sadly on the rise amongst teenagers. According to recent studies completed by a leading children's charity, 75% of young people with mental health problems are not accessing or receiving the help they so desperately need. This is extremely worrying but something we can work together on as a society.

I believe this book, which is full of tips and strategies, will provide relief and guidance to those who are currently struggling.

If you are reading this, then please remember - you are brave, you are strong, and you have got this!

Danielle Jenkins-Omar

Learning Mentor (SEMH) & Mental Health First Aider

B.A. (Hons) Childhood Studies

# Please Read

Please be aware that you may relate to some of the content in this book, and it might momentarily trigger some of your symptoms of anxiety. If you start to feel distressed, emotional, or become overwhelmed by the physical symptoms, thoughts, feelings, or behaviours of anxiety, please be kind to yourself and take a break. This book is here to provide comfort and relief, and there is no race to finish it. It is your companion. So, do read it, but read it at your own pace and in a space and moment that feels safe for you.

# Disclaimer

The advice in this book should not replace proper medical advice from your doctor. It should not serve as medical advice or any form of medical treatment. Please always speak to your doctor before changing anything to do with your medical treatment. If you are taking medications, do not stop or change this without consulting your doctor. This book has been written and published strictly for informational and educational purposes only. Not all of the advice in this book will be suitable for you, so please use it as informational only and not as a substitute for individual therapy or medical care.

*For any young person who has suffered, is suffering or may suffer.*

# Introduction

Hello!

If you are reading this book, it is probably because you are feeling anxious, you have suffered from anxiety or you would like to know more about anxiety.

Having anxiety can be extremely scary and worrying, but this book is here to help you.

It has lots of information and tips, and it will hopefully make what can be a difficult topic easier to understand.

Anxiety is a feeling of fear, worry and nervousness. These fears and worries often stem from something that has happened to you, something you have seen, heard, or been involved in during your life.

As horrible as it is though, anxiety is the result of a function that has kept humans alive since the dawn of time. You may have heard of the fight or flight response? This is a physiological reaction that we all feel when we sense danger, a threat to our lives, or an imminent attack.

This was great when we were running away from Saber-toothed Tigers in the Stone Age or for if our house or car is on fire right now. Rightly we would fight for our life or take flight and quickly. However, what has happened in the modern age with pressures, stresses, family dynamics and technology flying in from all angles, is that our fight or flight response has gone into overdrive. This has caused us to become overwhelmed by our anxieties and worries and develop symptoms that are horrendous and compromise our mental health.

If you think of your fight or flight response as your inbuilt fire alarm. You want it to go off if there is a genuine fire, but you do not want it to go off every time you make your toast in the morning. We need it for genuine emergencies, but we do not need it ringing in our ears all the time.

If we look back at the famed and now extinct bird, the Dodo, we can see why our inbuilt system is so important. The story has some variations to it, but the tale suggests when human sailors first reached the beautiful island of Mauritius, they came across the Dodo, which was a flightless bird a bit bigger than a Turkey. The Dodo was not scared of humans or their dogs as they had no natural predators and thus perceived no threat. They had no inbuilt fight or flight system and were therefore very easy to catch and eat and, as a result, became extinct.

This is a prime example of why we need our inbuilt alarm system, so we do not end up like the Dodo. However, we also do not want to feel full of fear, panic, be scared, and nervous all the time. Therefore, we need to find some peace in our lives.

Hopefully, this book will help you to understand anxiety a bit better and help you to manage your thoughts, feelings, and symptoms. Good luck.

(Excerpt is taken from 'Help with Anxiety')

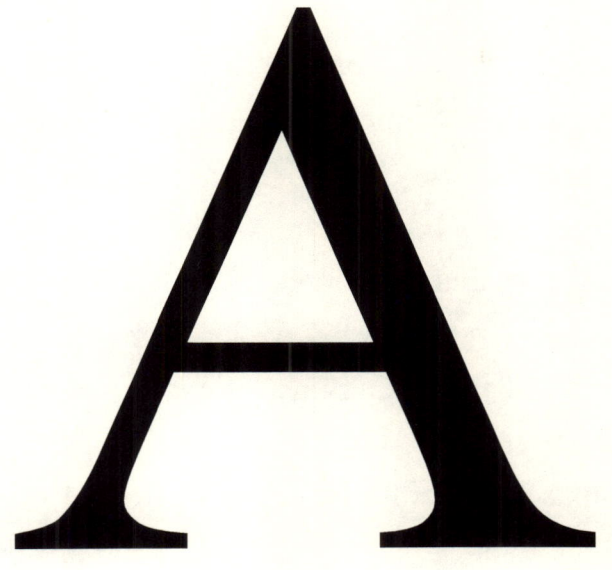

# IS FOR

# ANXIETY

# A is for Anxiety

## What is Anxiety?

Anxiety is a feeling of worry, fear or panic that can affect anyone regardless of their age, gender, where they live, how much money they have or what they look like. Some people might feel a little bit anxious, whereas some people might feel extremely anxious. A little bit of anxiety or worry can be completely normal in some circumstances. For example, if you are taking an exam, sitting a driving test, you have fallen out with your friends, or you are waiting for some results from the doctors. However, for some people, their anxious feelings can be present during times when they shouldn't be, and this can and have a negative effect on their everyday lives.

## How we experience anxiety can differ from one person to the next:

One thing is for sure. It can be terrifying; however, we experience it. You may not experience all of these symptoms, and there may be others that you do feel, but written below is a list of some of the most common. However, just because you experience some of them it does necessarily mean you have anxiety. It could be something else? So please speak to your parent/carer, teacher, or doctor about how you are feeling.

**YOU MAY FEEL**: Nervous, full of panic including panic attacks, on edge, scared, shaky, worried, like you're losing control, like you're going crazy, like you want to hurt yourself, like you might pass out, hyperaware, fatigued, tired, weak, breathless, tight chested, nauseous, hollow, detached, cold or hot, experience increased heart rate and heart palpitations, struggle sleeping (insomnia), rapid breathing or hyperventilation, diarrhoea, intrusive thoughts, a dry mouth, digestive problems, aches and pains, sweating, being overly aware of your heartbeat, repetitive thoughts, negative thoughts, obsessions and compulsions amongst other things.

## What types of anxiety disorders are there?

**General Anxiety Disorder (GAD)** – This means you worry regularly and uncontrollably. GAD symptoms are extremely broad, which means the way you experience it might slightly differ from someone else.

**Social Anxiety Disorder** – This means you experience intense fear in social situations like school, parties, sports events and more. You might worry about what will happen or about what people might think of you, say to you, or do to you.

**Panic Disorder** – This means you experience regular panic attacks without a known reason or trigger. The thought of having a panic attack can also trigger you into having a panic attack.

**Phobias, including Agoraphobia** – This means you experience extreme fear or panic as you believe a situation or object might hurt you. For example, being scared of heights, open or enclosed spaces, public transport, spiders or snakes.

**Post-Traumatic Stress Disorder (PTSD)** – This might develop after experiencing a traumatic event in your life. You may experience nightmares or flashbacks to the event in question.

**Obsessive-Compulsive Disorder (OCD)** – This means you obsessively (do something a lot) think about something, or perform an action or urge, i.e. washing your hands twenty times or thinking your parents might die if you do not switch the light on and off. You may also suffer from unwanted, upsetting, and intrusive thoughts that you obsessively think about.

**Health Anxiety** – This means you experience anxiety and obsessions around your health and may regularly check or Google your symptoms or visit your doctor to see if you are okay.

**Separation Anxiety** – This means you experience excessive worry about being away from a certain person, place or pet.

**Body Dysmorphic Disorder (BDD)** – This means you worry about the way you look and appear. This may be through your weight, body or facial appearance, clothing, or something else.

## What should you do if you think you have an anxiety disorder?

If you experience any of the above symptoms or think you may have an anxiety disorder, then you should speak to one or more of the following:

- Your parent/s or carer/s.
- Your doctor.
- Your teacher/s.
- Your family and/or friends.
- Someone you trust.

- One of the specialist organisations in the Other Support section of this book.

Write down the things that make you feel anxious. Then once you have written them down, make sure to speak to someone you trust about them:

...................................................................

...................................................................

...................................................................

...................................................................

...................................................................

...................................................................

...................................................................

...................................................................

...................................................................

...................................................................

...................................................................

...................................................................

# IS FOR

# BREATHING

# B is for Breathing

## What does breathing have to do with anxiety?

There are two ways to look at this. Firstly, having anxiety can sometimes affect your breathing. It can make your breathing fast and shallow instead of calm and deep, especially as you enter a panic attack. As this gets worse and you cannot stop your spiralling thoughts of anxiety, you may hyperventilate. This is just a fancy word that means you exhale (breathe out) more than you inhale (breathe in). Hyperventilating is likely to increase your feelings of anxiousness as you can become lightheaded, feel a tingling sensation in your body and feel your heart rate increasing.

## HOWEVER....

....all is not doom and gloom. This brings us on to the second way of looking at breathing and anxiety. Learning to control our breathing both during a panic attack and during normal everyday life can have a positive effect on our anxiety and general wellbeing. So, let's have a look at some breathing techniques that could help you.

**Breathing techniques, we can try to help keep us calm.**

- These can be done anywhere, any time and any place. Try practising them and see how you feel.
- Make sure you are sat or lay comfortably.
- If you want to close your eyes, you can do (but you do not have to).
- Do not worry if you cannot reach the maximum number of breaths to begin with; just do as much as you feel comfortable with. Everyone is different.

..........

**Deep Breathing** – Try breathing in through your nose and then out through your mouth for up to 4 seconds each way. Breathe in through the nose, counting in your head 1,2,3,4 and then out through the mouth 1,2,3,4. Make sure you are sat or lay comfortably when you do this, and try to do it for a couple of minutes. Don't worry if you can only reach 3 seconds at first; you will improve the more you do it.

**478 Breathing** – To try this technique, breathe in through your nose for 4 seconds, hold your breath in for 7 seconds and then breath out for up to 8 seconds. Then repeat this exercise for a couple of minutes.

**Box Breathing** – Also known as 4x4 breathing, this technique is used by athletes and celebrities to help them focus quickly. To try this, breathe in through the nose for 4 seconds, then hold your breath in for 4 seconds. Then you should breathe out through your mouth for 4 seconds before holding your exhaled breath for 4 seconds. Repeat this process for a couple of minutes.

**Belly Breathing** – Lying down, put one hand on your belly and one hand on your chest. Take a deep breath in for 4 seconds and feel your belly moving outwards. Then breathe out slowly through your mouth for 4 seconds, lightly pushing on your belly. Repeat this exercise for a couple of minutes.

## Did you know?

Deep breathing not only helps your body to feel calmer but by concentrating on it, it can also help to distract your mind away from any anxious thoughts you may be having.

# C

## IS FOR

## CAUSES

# C is for Causes

## What causes anxiety?

There is no one answer to this question as anxiety can be very different from one person to the next. However, there are some key factors that can influence how and why anxiety may occur within us. We will look at these more in-depth on the next page, but briefly, these are:

**Your Genetics** – These are the biological traits you share with your parents, grandparents, and other family members.

**Your Current Life** – These are the things that are going on in your life right now that might make you feel anxious.

**Stress** – These are the things that cause you stress in your life.

**Past Experiences** – These are things that might have happened in your past that make you feel anxious.

**Childhood Experiences** – These are things that might have happened during your childhood that make you feel anxious.

**Physical Health Problems** – These are physical health problems that you may be suffering from that are making you feel anxious.

**Mental Health Problems** – Anxiety can be a symptom of lots of other mental health conditions.

**Medication** – Anxiety can be a side-effect of some medications.

**Illegal Drugs** – Anxiety can be a side-effect of taking illegal drugs.

..........

**Anxiety disorders can develop from a complicated set of factors, including your genes, body chemistry, life events and more.**

**It can affect anyone, anywhere, anyplace, anytime.**

..........

Here are some questions to answer when thinking about why you might be suffering from anxiety:

**Your Genetics** – Do your parents or grandparents suffer from anxiety, depression, or any other mental health illness?

**Your Current Life** – What is going on in your life right now? Are you worried about school? Your family? Your friends? Money? Your future? Or is something happening that makes you feel uneasy?

**Stress** – Are there things in your life that make you feel stressed? If so, what are they? This could be things to do with your family, friends, school, or something else.

**Past Experiences** – Has something happened in your past that still upsets you? Have you spoken to someone about it? Has something happened to you that you could not control? This could be to do with a person or a situation.

**Childhood Experiences** – Has something happened in your childhood that still upsets you? Have you spoken to someone about it? Has something happened to you that you could not control? This could be to do with a person or a situation.

**Physical Health Problems** – Do you suffer from any known physical health problems? Do you have any temporary or permanent injuries?

**Mental Health problems** – Do you suffer from any known mental health problems?

**Medication** – Are you taking any prescribed medication for anything? If so, is anxiety a known side-effect?

**Illegal Drugs** – Have you ever taken illegal drugs? Are you currently taking illegal drugs?

**Notes:**

..........................................................................

..........................................................................

..........................................................................

..........................................................................

..........................................................................

..........................................................................

..........................................................................

..........................................................................

..........................................................................

..........................................................................

..........................................................................

..........................................................................

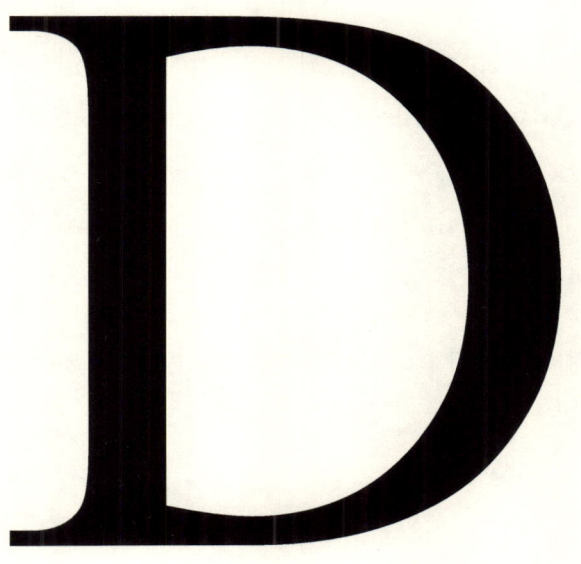

# IS FOR

# DIET

# D is for Diet

## How can what I eat and drink affect anxiety?

What does the word diet mean to you? Does it remind you of people eating salads for weeks before they go on their summer holidays? Or maybe people drinking fruit smoothies every day? Well, it is all those things, but basically it is:

### The food and drink normally consumed by an individual.

This means that it is not just about dieting to lose or gain weight, but it is actually about EVERYTHING that you eat and drink. Importantly, what you eat, and drink can affect the way you feel, your emotions, the way you look and your energy levels. That is why it is extremely important to consume the right foods and drinks to maintain a healthily balanced body.

One of the things that your diet can affect is… you've got it….anxiety! Some foods and drinks are good for anxiety, and then there are some real nasties that are bad for it.

## So, what are they?

Well, let us start with some of the nasties:

**Processed Sugars:** As much as everyone loves foods packed with processed sugar, they can make you feel more anxious after consuming them. Foods and drinks full of processed sugars include chocolate, cakes, sweets, fizzy drinks, fruit juices, biscuits, some yoghurts and many more. Yes, all the best ones! The reason they can make you feel more anxious is that they affect something in your body called your blood sugars. Eating them can make your blood sugars rush up high, but what goes up must come down. When your blood sugars drop, this can make you feel irritable and tense, which can make your symptoms of anxiety feel even worse. This does not make everyone anxious, but it is worth remembering if you are suffering from anxiety.

**Caffeine:** Another nasty for anxiety is caffeine. Products that might contain caffeine include coffee, energy drinks, tea, dark chocolate, full-sugar cola's, other similar soft drinks, some medications and more. Caffeine can be bad for people with anxiety. It can stimulate our body's natural flight or fight response, which can make your anxiety feel worse and even trigger an anxiety attack. If you must have these, do not overdo them.

**Alcohol:** Now, you should not be drinking alcohol until you are over 18 years old in the U.K. and over 21 years old in the USA. However, just for the record, drinking alcohol can lead to you feeling extremely anxious the next day. It alters your levels of serotonin and disturbs your neurotransmitters. This can lead to an increase in anxious feelings once the effects of alcohol wear off. Its hangovers can lead to dehydration, an unbalanced brain, low blood sugars and an increased heart rate - all a melting pot of nasties for anyone who already suffers from anxiety.

## So, what is good for anxiety?

**Water:** Studies have shown that when our body is dehydrated, it does not function as well as it should. Blood pressure may drop, which can lead to dizziness and a faster heartbeat as the heart tries to increase low blood pressure. This can all lead to bringing on a panic attack. The recommended intake of fluids is 6-8 glasses a day.

**Fruit:** There are lots of fruits that have a positive effect on anxiety. These include bananas, which are a cheap and awesome source of energy, rich in tryptophan. This is an amino acid responsible for inducing serotonin and relaxation in our bodies. Pineapple has also been shown to have a positive impact on the body. It contains an enzyme called bromelain which may help to lower stress.

**Eggs:** Another food containing tryptophan is eggs, so these are good to add into the diet.

**Broccoli:** Broccoli and celery are both a natural source of potassium and folic acid. Studies have shown that both have anti-anxiety qualities.

**Remember, you can enjoy all foods – just everything in moderation.**

. . . . . . . . . .

**You should also eat meals regularly and try not to skip or miss meals because:**

Eating healthy balanced meals regularly (i.e. breakfast, lunch, tea & supper) helps to keep your blood sugar levels stabilised. If your blood sugar levels are not stabilised, then they can make your body feel like it is going through a sugary roller-coaster with great highs and shaky, nervous lows. Skipping just one meal or waiting too long between meals can cause your blood sugar levels to drop. This can make you feel super anxious.

Write down your favourite foods and decide if they help your anxiety or could make it worse.

| Good For Anxiety | Might Be Bad For Anxiety |
|---|---|
|  |  |
|  |  |
|  |  |
|  |  |
|  |  |
|  |  |
|  |  |
|  |  |
|  |  |
|  |  |
|  |  |
|  |  |

# IS FOR

# EXERCISE

# E is for Exercise

## What is exercise?

Exercise is physical activity that you can do to help your body become healthier, fitter and stronger. Sounds good, doesn't it? Well, the best news of all is that exercise is brilliant for anxiety… but why? Well, exercise produces endorphins in the body that act as a natural pain killer. These stimulate anti-anxiety effects and improve our ability to sleep. Exercise will reward you both physically and mentally. It will also help to boost your confidence and self-esteem too.

## So, what types of exercise can you do?

- Running
- Swimming
- Football
- Athletics
- Gymnastics
- Boxing
- Rugby
- Dancing
- Cycling

- Basketball
- Weightlifting
- Tennis
- Fitness Classes
- Yoga
- And many many more....

Write down here some exercises that you have tried and like?

...............................................................................

...............................................................................

...............................................................................

...............................................................................

...............................................................................

...............................................................................

**Whether you exercise already or have never exercised in your life, here is a plan to help you along your way. Planning can help us to manage our anxiety and can be extremely useful to our lives. You should aim to exercise at least 3-4 times a week for 20-30 minutes.**

- **MONDAY**

  Will you exercise today? i.e. Yes

  What will you do? i.e. Swimming

  What time will you do this? i.e. 6pm

  How long for? i.e. 1 hour

  ..............................................................

  ..............................................................

  ..............................................................

- **TUESDAY**

  Will you exercise today?

  What will you do?

  What time will you do this?

  How long for?

  ..............................................................

  ..............................................................

  ..............................................................

- **WEDNESDAY**

  Will you exercise today?

  What will you do?

  What time will you do this?

  How long for?

  ..............................................................

  ..............................................................

  ..............................................................

- **THURSDAY**

  Will you exercise today?

  What will you do?

  What time will you do this?

  How long for?

  ....................................................................

  ....................................................................

  ....................................................................

- **FRIDAY**

  Will you exercise today?

  What will you do?

  What time will you do this?

  How long for?

  ....................................................................

  ....................................................................

  ....................................................................

- **SATURDAY**

  Will you exercise today?

  What will you do?

  What time will you do this?

  How long for?

  ....................................................................

  ....................................................................

  ....................................................................

- **SUNDAY**

  Will you exercise today?

  What will you do?

  What time will you do this?

  How long for?

  ...................................................................

  ...................................................................

  ...................................................................

**Notes:**

...................................................................

...................................................................

...................................................................

...................................................................

...................................................................

...................................................................

...................................................................

...................................................................

...................................................................

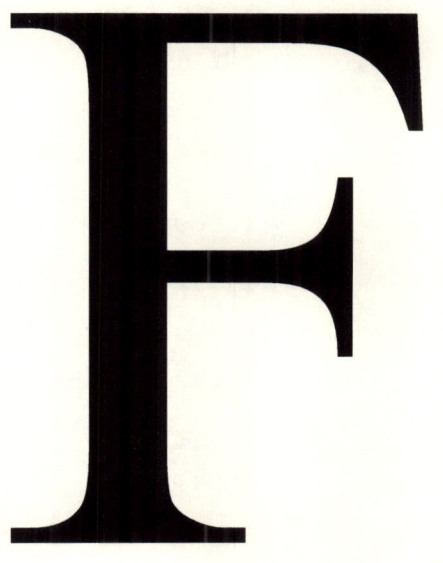

# IS FOR

# FEAR

# F is for Fear

**What is fear?**

Fear plays a huge role in anxiety. It is an emotion that makes us worried or scared of something, someone or a situation. Usually, as we believe something bad will happen to us as a result. Maybe you are scared of going to school? Maybe you are scared of seeing a certain person? Maybe you are scared of your parents dying? Maybe you are scared of spiders or heights? Maybe you are worried about being rejected, embarrassed, letting people down or failing at something?

A little bit of fear can be normal, but when it starts to rule our lives and our feelings, then it could develop into anxiety.

List some things here that make you feel worried or fearful:

.............................................................

.............................................................

.............................................................

Now, thinking about what you have written, can you remember why these things fill you with fear? Has something happened in your past, or have you seen something on T.V. or social media? Write them down here.

...................................................................

...................................................................

...................................................................

...................................................................

**So, how can we manage our fears? Here are some exercises to try and help you.**

**Talk About Your Fears** – If you are worried and anxious about something, then make sure to talk to someone you trust about how you are feeling. Remember, a problem shared is a problem halved.

**Face Your Fears** – If you feel comfortable, you could try facing your fears. Are you scared of spiders? Try looking at pictures of spiders, then getting close to a spider, then touching a spider and so on. Slowly face your fears until you are less scared of them.

**Distraction Techniques** – To manage your fears, you could try something called distraction techniques. These are where you distract your mind from your fears. For example, if you start feeling anxious about something, try and count from 1-50 in your head and then back down again. Or try and think of the words to your favourite song and sing it in your head or out loud. This will replace your negative thoughts with the thoughts you are concentrating on.

**Relax** – There is a whole section on relaxation in this book, but if you are feeling full of fear, you should try and relax. You could do this by listening to music, reading a book, talking to your friends, playing with a pet or something else.

**Understand And Accept** – It is important to understand why you feel the way you do and not be scared of it. The more you understand why you feel the way you do, the less control your fears and anxieties will have over you.

**Picture A Happy Place** – Try and refocus your thoughts on something happy. Maybe this is somewhere you have been, or somewhere you would like to go.

**FACT** - A recent report revealed that for girls between the ages of 11 to 16 years old, nearly two thirds who had a probable mental disorder had experienced seeing or hearing an adult argument in their household.

**QUESTION** – What might a girl who has seen or heard an argument be fearful of? Could this make her more anxious?

..................................................................

..................................................................

..................................................................

..................................................................

..................................................................

..................................................................

..................................................................

..................................................................

..................................................................

..................................................................

..................................................................

..................................................................

..................................................................

..................................................................

# IS FOR

# GROUNDING

# G is for Grounding

## What is grounding?

Grounding (in this book) is not what your parents or carers do to you when you have been naughty. What it is, though, with anxiety, is a task or technique you can perform to help bring you back down to earth (ground you) when you are feeling anxious or having a panic attack.

## Does grounding work?

Yes! There are lots of studies and case studies that suggest grounding techniques work. They can help people with anxiety to become less anxious and move away from a having panic attack.

## Grounding techniques to try:

**The Alphabet Game** - The next time you are feeling anxious or worried about something, try this technique. Starting with A, think of a person's name, a place and an animal beginning with the letter A. Then, once you have done that move on to B, then C and so on. This should help to refocus your attention away from your anxious thoughts.

**54321 Method** - The 54321 method is another grounding technique that works like the Alphabet Game. To try this, you should think of or say five things you can see around you, four things you can touch, three things you can hear, two things you can smell and one thing you can taste.

**Listen To Music** - As mentioned in the L section of this book, listening to music can help to ground you and decrease your feelings of anxiety.

**Breathing Techniques** - Try using the breathing techniques shown in this book to help ground you. You can also use the breathing techniques whilst going through the other methods too.

**Google Jokes** - Sounds funny? Well, that is the aim. Try Googling jokes that will make you laugh. Reading them can help to refocus your mind and ground you. Additionally, laughter has also been shown to increase your serotonin levels, also known as your happy hormones.

**Focus On An Activity** - Is there something you like doing? This could be reading, playing a game on your phone, drawing, writing or something else. Whatever it is, focus your attention on that when you feel anxious. That way, you can do something fun instead of just sitting or standing there feeling anxious.

**Listen To The Sounds Of Nature -** There are lots of apps you can get on your phone that will play sounds of nature. There will also be videos you can listen to and watch on YouTube. Studies have shown that listening to sounds of nature can help our bodies to relax, decreasing anxiety and promoting relaxation.

**Drawing Or Colouring -** Drawing or colouring can help you refocus your attention and make you feel more relaxed.

## Have you tried any of the grounding techniques listed?

If so, which ones?

..................................................................................

..................................................................................

..................................................................................

..................................................................................

Which ones worked the best for you?

...................................................................

...................................................................

...................................................................

...................................................................

...................................................................

...................................................................

...................................................................

...................................................................

...................................................................

...................................................................

...................................................................

...................................................................

...................................................................

...................................................................

...................................................................

# H

## IS FOR HELPING OTHERS

# H is for Helping Others

**How can we help others who might be feeling anxious?**

As well as us feeling anxious, our family and friends might experience anxiety too. Therefore, it is always good to know how you can help other people if they feel anxious or experience a panic attack.

**How to help someone experiencing anxiety:**

- If someone opens up to you about feeling anxious, then be kind and understanding.
- If you feel like someone may be experiencing anxiety but hasn't mentioned it to you, you can always ask if they would like to talk to you. However, do not pressurise them and be patient with them.
- If they do speak to you, then you could follow the 5 Step Plan.

**5 Step Plan - ALASK**

1.) **Ask** them what it is they are anxious about. Be kind, patient and understanding.

2.) **Listen** to what they have to say. Be non-judgemental and comforting.

3.) **Ask** them how you can help them.

4.) **Suggest** they speak to someone who can help – this can be a parent, teacher, doctor, counsellor or someone else.

5.) **Keep** in touch and find out if they managed to get help. Support them as much as you can.

..........

## How would you help?

Read the following case studies and decide how you might help each person.

## Case Study 1 – Jessica

Jessica is 14 years old. She tells you that she is really worried that people do not like her. She is so worried that sometimes she doesn't sleep at night, and she thinks about it all of the time. She thinks people do not like her because someone once wrote something mean on social media about her. She tells you that sometimes she gets short of breath and dizzy if she thinks about it too much.

How could you help Jessica?

..............................................................................

..............................................................................

..............................................................................

..............................................................................

## Case Study 2 – Carlos

Carlos is 15 years old. You have noticed that whenever family issues are discussed in a lesson, he leaves the classroom to go to the toilet. You can see through the classroom door that when he gets outside, he is holding his chest like he is having a panic attack. After a while, he comes back in, and the teacher asks him if he is okay. He always says he is. You have a feeling that something is not right, but Carlos hasn't mentioned anything to you.

How could you help Carlos?

..............................................................................

..............................................................................

..............................................................................

..............................................................................

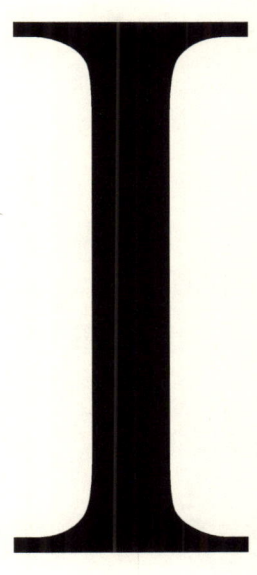

# IS FOR ILLEGAL
# DRUGS

# I is for Illegal Drugs

## What are illegal drugs?

Drugs are substances that affect the way our body's function. There are two classifications of drugs – legal and illegal. Legal drugs might also be known as prescription drugs or medication. These are the type you might get from the doctor or hospital to help make you feel better or manage an illness. Illegal drugs, on the other hand, are substances that are prohibited by law because of their potential to cause serious harm. They might also be called recreational drugs.

## What types of illegal drugs are there?

There are lots of illegal drugs, including:

- Ecstasy and MDMA
- Cocaine
- Amphetamines, e.g. Speed
- Ketamine
- Heroin
- Spice
- LSD

- GHB
- Steroids
- Cannabis (UK)
- Balloons (Nitrous Oxide)
- Fentanyl
- M-CAT, Crack and many more.

## Why are illegal drugs bad?

Taking illegal drugs can have short term and long-term impacts on your physical and mental health. The types of drugs taken and the length of time they are taken can all play a role. However, even taking them just once can have a damaging effect.

## Here are some of the side effects of illegal drugs:

- Panic Attacks
- Anxiety
- Dizziness
- Loss of Consciousness
- Paranoia
- High Blood Pressure
- Feeling Sick
- Hallucinations
- Feeling Drowsy

- Memory Problems
- Shaking
- Sweating
- Diarrhoea
- Depression
- Fear
- Nightmares
- Overdose
- Heart Attack

**Some shocking statistics!**

There are many, many more side effects, including, sadly death. Research and reports have suggested that in England and Wales in 2019 there were over 4,000 drug poisoning deaths. This was the highest number since statistics started being recorded in 1993. Reports have also shown that there has been over a 50% increase in deaths related to drugs over the last decade. Some scary stats. Additionally, illegal drugs can also have a serious impact on someone's mental health.

**What are the effects of taking drugs on anxiety?**

Taking illegal drugs can make you feel anxious while taking them, or for days, weeks, months and even years afterwards. They can also give you panic attacks while taking them or for a long time afterwards. This is because illegal drugs can alter the chemicals in your brain and trigger feelings of anxiousness and other similar symptoms. They can make you feel worried, scared, paranoid, dizzy and drowsy. They can also make your heart race faster and senses more heightened. These are all similar symptoms of anxiety disorders. So, you can see why taking them can lead to developing anxiety or making it worse.

If you already have anxiety, then taking drugs is highly likely to make it even worse. If you have never taken them, then do not start, as you may develop anxiety as a result, or another mental or physical health problem. If you are feeling pressured by friends or family into taking drugs, then speak to a responsible adult who you trust. Nobody should make you feel bad or force you into doing something that can affect your health.

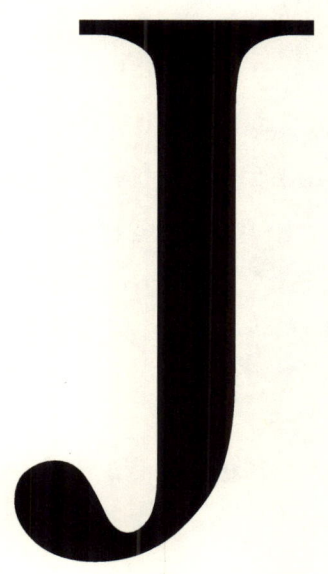

# IS FOR

# JOURNAL

# J is for Journal

## What is a journal?

A journal is somewhere you can keep a record of the things that happen in your daily life. Also known as a diary, a journal can help you to identify the things that make you feel more anxious and the things that help you have a better day. At the end of each day, you should write down a few sentences about what has happened and how you felt. For example:

*Today was a good day. I did some exercise and ate healthily. I saw my friends, and I watched my favourite programme on Netflix. I also spent some time listening to relaxing music and doing some breathing exercises. I didn't feel so anxious today.*

If after a few days of journaling like this, you might suggest that on days when you exercise and eat healthier, you feel less anxious. You might also note that on days you see your friends and watch your favourite programme you feel happier. Furthermore, you might note that when you do breathing exercises and listen to certain songs, you feel more relaxed.

Let's have a look at a bad day…

*Today was a bad day, and I felt really anxious. I fell out with my friend, which made me upset, and I heard my mum and dad arguing. I ate lots of sugary sweets and drank an energy drink.*

If you have written similar things a few times in your journal, you might conclude that you feel more anxious on days where you fall out with your friends or hear your mum and dad arguing. You might also find that when you eat lots of sugary foods and consume energy drinks, you feel irritable, which makes your anxiety worse.

Looking at these examples, it is easy to see how keeping a journal can help you to notice the things that make your anxiety better and the things that make your anxiety worse.

## On the following pages, write down how you feel for the next few days.

Think about how anxious you feel or how good you feel. Write down what you eat and drink, if you do any exercise, if anything happens that makes you worried or upset or if you did anything to help improve your wellbeing.

# DAY 1

..................................................................................

..................................................................................

..................................................................................

..................................................................................

# DAY 2

..................................................................................

..................................................................................

..................................................................................

..................................................................................

# DAY 3

..................................................................................

..................................................................................

..................................................................................

..................................................................................

**If you find that keeping a journal works well for you, then ask your parents, carers, or teachers to provide you with a journal or diary so you can keep using one.**

## MOOD TRACKER

Another strategy that is like a journal is a Mood Tracker. A Mood Tracker can help you identify trends in your anxiety as you colour in days on a calendar depending on how you felt that day. Below is an example of this. If you would like to try a Mood Tracker, there are lots available online or ask an adult to help you get one.

**A Weekly Mood Tracker**

|  | Monday | Tuesday | Wednesday | Thursday | Friday | Saturday | Sunday |
|---|---|---|---|---|---|---|---|
| Morning | △ | ○ | ■ | ■ | ■ | ○ | ○ |
| Afternoon | △ | ○ | ■ | ■ | ○ | ○ | ○ |
| Evening | △ | △ | △ | △ | ○ | ○ | △ |

○ Felt Great    ■ Felt Meh!    △ Felt Anxious

If this was your Mood Tracker you would be able to identify the following:

- You feel anxious on Monday.

63

- You feel anxious in the evenings.
- You feel great at the weekend.
- You feel meh in the middle of the week.

By knowing this information, you should then start to identify why you feel more anxious in the evenings and on Monday and why you feel great at the weekend. This should help you to manage your anxiety.

**Notes:**

...........................................................................

...........................................................................

...........................................................................

...........................................................................

...........................................................................

...........................................................................

...........................................................................

...........................................................................

...........................................................................

...........................................................................

# IS FOR

# KINDNESS

# K is for Kindness

**Be kind to yourself.**

If you are suffering from anxiety, then you need to be kind to yourself. Struggling with fears and worries can be extremely difficult, so we need to take time to look after our mental health. Here are some things to remember:

- If you have a bad day, tomorrow could be better – be kind to yourself.
- If you mess up, you can always make amends – be kind to yourself.
- If you think you have failed at something, you can always try again – be kind to yourself.
- If you think you have let someone down, you can always make it up – be kind to yourself.
- If you think you have let yourself down, life is a learning curve – be kind to yourself.
- Get the picture?

Life can be difficult enough without us adding extra pressure and stress onto ourselves. On the next page, we will look at some strategies to help you be kinder to yourself.

# How can you be kind to yourself?

**Make Time For Yourself** – Find time in the day to do things that make you happy. That might be a hobby, seeing friends or something else.

**Believe in Yourself** – Have faith in yourself and your own abilities and believe that you can achieve anything.

**Accept Yourself** – Appreciate that you may not be perfect (nobody is) but that you have some amazing qualities and strengths.

**Recognise Your Successes** – You should feel great about the things in your life that are good and the things that you have achieved, whether that is a certificate, an award, or even getting through a bad time.

**Forgive Yourself** – If you feel you have done something wrong in the past, do not beat yourself up over it. Learn from it, forgive yourself and move on.

**Take Care Of Yourself** – Eat healthily, exercise, sleep well and look after yourself and your body.

**Respect Yourself** – Have faith in yourself, your opinions, and your abilities. Appreciate when you are wrong but stand up for what you feel is right.

**Treat Yourself** – If you have some pocket money, then treat yourself to something you like. Or maybe just treat yourself to a slice of cake for working hard at school.

**Relax** – Take time to relax. See the relaxation section in this book.

..........

## Be kind to other people.

As well as being kind to yourself, you should always be kind to other people too. Just like you might be going through a difficult time, you never know what other people are going through or how they are feeling.

Recent reports have suggested that 1 in 10 young people between the ages of 11 to 22 years old reported that they felt lonely. Additionally, it has also been reported by a leading mental health charity that 1 in 5 young people might experience a mental health illness during any given year. These statistics show that a lot of people are going through a difficult time. If there are 30 people in your class, then at least three people might be feeling lonely, and six people might experience a mental health problem throughout the year.

## So, how can you be kind to others?

1. Be nice to those around you – a smile and a 'How are you?' can go a long way.
2. Do not be mean to people – do not call someone names, make fun of them or bully them.
3. Try to speak to people you believe might be experiencing some sort of difficulty.
4. If someone opens up to you, be empathetic – a fancy word for showing that you understand how they are feeling.
5. Do not be judgemental of others – you never know what someone is going through.

## Notes:

..............................................................................

..............................................................................

..............................................................................

..............................................................................

..............................................................................

..............................................................................

..............................................................................

# IS FOR LISTEN

# L is for Listen

**Listen to music.**

Studies have shown that listening to music can help to reduce feelings of anxiety by up to 65%. Of course, this does depend on the type of music you are listening to. There will be songs that make you feel happy, songs that make you feel sad, songs that make you feel angry and songs that make you cry.

If you are suffering from anxiety, you should try and listen to music that makes you feel happy or relaxed. This music will be unique to you but may include your favourite singers, bands, D.J.'s and more.

You can make your own playlists on YouTube, Amazon Music, Spotify and many more.

You could also try typing relaxing music into these platforms and seeing what comes up. There are thousands of relaxing songs out there that might help to ease your anxiety, so get looking.

On the next page, we are going to make our Anxiety Be Calm Playlist.

**Write down all your favourite songs that make you feel happy or relaxed. Then make a playlist and listen to them whenever you feel anxious.**

## Anxiety Be Calm Playlist

**Song 1**

....................................................................

**Song 2**

....................................................................

**Song 3**

....................................................................

**Song 4**

....................................................................

**Song 5**

....................................................................

**Song 6**

....................................................................

**Song 7**

....................................................................

**Song 8**

....................................................................

**Song 9**

...................................................................

**Song 10**

...................................................................

## Sounds of nature.

Just like listening to music can help to reduce feelings of anxiety, so can listening to the sounds of nature. Studies have shown that it can lower levels of our stress hormone cortisol.

The next time you feel anxious, try walking in the garden, in the park or somewhere peaceful and listen to the sounds of the birds, the bees and the breeze.

Alternatively, there are several apps available that will play sounds of nature, and there are also playlists available on YouTube and other streaming services. Whether you are at home, on your break at school or somewhere else, the next time you feel your anxiety levels rising, try listening to the sounds of nature.

Write down here the sounds of nature that help you to relax.

# Sounds of nature playlist.

**Sound 1**

......................................................................

**Sound 2**

......................................................................

**Sound 3**

......................................................................

**Sound 4**

......................................................................

**Sound 5**

......................................................................

**Notes:**

......................................................................

......................................................................

......................................................................

......................................................................

......................................................................

......................................................................

......................................................................

# M

## IS FOR

## MINDFULNESS

# M is for Mindfulness

## What is mindfulness?

Mindfulness is the state in which we are aware and pay attention to the present moment. This includes focussing on our own thoughts, feelings and the world around us. It is a form of meditation that can help us to relax our body and mind, increase our happiness and help us to cope better with our anxieties and worries.

It is believed that by mindfully meditating, you can improve your mental wellbeing.

## Sounds a bit hippy, right?

Well, maybe so, but it can really help people to cope with their mental health. It can be as simple as listening to the birds in the trees, feeling the wind on your face or smelling a beautiful Sunday meal cooking in the kitchen.

## So, what should you do?

One way we can practice being mindful is by just sitting in silence with no distractions for a few minutes. Focus on your breathing using one of the breathing techniques in this book. Then think about how you have been feeling and how you have been behaving.

Try and allow yourself to become familiar with your anxious thoughts without becoming scared by them or judging them, good or bad. This will enable you to address your anxiety more calmly.

On the following pages, we will look at some techniques that can help you to practice mindfulness.

## Mindfulness Techniques

**Mindful Breathing** - To practice mindfully breathing, find a quiet spot, close your eyes, and try one of the breathing techniques in this book. Do this for a couple of minutes and think about how you have been feeling.

**Mindful Walking** - To practice mindfully walking, go for a walk somewhere relaxing like the park, countryside, beach or somewhere else. Do not listen to music and put your phone away. Just focus on the sights and sounds around you and enjoy the relaxing surroundings.

**Mindful Colouring** - To practice colouring mindfully, get a colouring book and just sit and colour in silence. As simple as that. Enjoy and relax the meditative state that colouring and drawing can create. Allow your thoughts to pass in and out.

**Mindful Listening** - To practice mindfully listening, you can either listen to relaxing music or the sounds of nature. Listen to the music, the sounds, the noises and let your thoughts come and go.

**Mindful Sitting** - To practice mindfully sitting, all you need to do is sit in silence. Focus on your surroundings and just relax.

**Mindful Bubbles** - To practice mindful bubbles, all you need to do is blow bubbles, like the ones you would get from the shop. Just enjoy blowing them and watching them float through the air and popping as they land.

**Mindful Exercise** - To practice mindfully exercising, focus on the exercise you are doing, whether that's swimming, running, yoga or something else.

# IS FOR

# NEGATIVE

# THINKING

# <u>N is for Negative Thinking</u>

## What is negative thinking?

Negative thinking and negative thoughts are where you think negatively about yourself, those around you, your surroundings, or the things you have done or might have to do.

Examples of negative thinking and thoughts are:

"I hate myself."

"I am going to fail."

"What's the point? Nothing good ever happens to me."

"People think I'm ugly and fat".

"I'm always going to be miserable."

Now, we ALL have negative thoughts from time to time. But if your negative thoughts are present all the time and affecting your life, then it is something you need to try and work on.

## So, why does negative thinking occur?

Negative thinking occurs…because we are human, and our brains are extremely complex. We react to situations differently, and we are formed by the things that have happened to us in our past, our genes and other external factors. You probably know someone that's always energetic and really positive, right? And then someone that's always down and gloomy. Well, those two people have probably had very different journeys in life. Or maybe they haven't, and that's just the way they are. Whatever your journey, your genetics, or the life you live, you will experience negative thoughts.

## But what can we do to stop these negative thoughts from ruling our world?

**Talk About How You Are Feeling** – This is a key theme throughout this book as it is super important. Do not keep your negative thoughts bottled up, as that will not be good for you. Instead, share them with someone you trust.

**Recognise** – It is important to recognise when we are thinking negatively. If we find ourselves thinking negatively and caught in a spiral of worry or fear, then we need to check-in with ourselves and stop. You can say

"Stop" in your mind if this helps. This is called thought stopping.

**Acknowledge And Move On** – We are going to experience negative thoughts. The trick is not to pay too much attention to them. If they come into your head, acknowledge them as a negative thought and quickly move on. Do not pay them any more attention than they deserve.

**Positive Affirmations** – Something extremely popular nowadays is positive affirmations. This is where you practice saying positive words and sayings every day until you believe them. Examples might be "I am happy", "I am a good person", "I feel healthy", "I am excited about the future", and so on.

**Distraction Techniques** – You could try distraction techniques like the ones mentioned in this book. Good ones include the 54321 method and the Alphabet Game.

**Just Do Something** – If you find yourself overthinking negatively, do not just sit or stand there and let it take over you. Change your thought process by doing something. Do anything. Just do something other than thinking negatively.

**Write & Destroy** – You could try writing down your negative thoughts and then throwing them in the bin. Once you have done this, make a promise to yourself to use the techniques above to think more positively going forward.

## ACTIVITY

**Write down some examples of negatives thoughts you may have had before. Or that someone might have.**

**1.)**

.........................................................

**2.)**

.........................................................

**3.)**

.........................................................

**4.)**

.........................................................

**5.)**

.........................................................

**Using the techniques above, think about how you could deal with these negative thoughts if you experience them again.**

# IS FOR OTHER
# SUPPORT

# O is for Other Support

**In this chapter, we will look at what other support is out there to help you with your anxiety.**

Along with learning to help yourself, where else can you turn to? Here is a list of people you could and should talk to if you need to:

**Your Parents Or Carers**: Hopefully, you feel like you can speak to your parents and carers. They should be able to introduce you to other services or ask your school for help. However, if this is not possible, then you can work your way through the list below.

**Your Friends**: Your friends can be a great source of support for you. If you feel comfortable talking to your friends and trust them, then make sure to talk together about how you are feeling.

**Speak To Your Doctor**: Your doctor will be a great person to speak to as they can tell you about all the services available to help you. Your doctor will see hundreds if not thousands of people a year with similar problems. So do not feel ashamed to speak to them.

**Teachers**: If you get along with a certain teacher or member of staff at your school, then you could speak to them. They will be able to help you and provide you with the support you need in school. Remember that the teacher may have experienced anxiety in their life before and most probably know people that do. So do not feel silly or scared speaking to them.

**Counsellors**: Following on from speaking to any of the above people, you may be referred to speak to a counsellor. Seeing a counsellor is nothing to be worried about. In fact, it should be of great benefit to your life. A counsellor can work with you through several approaches to help you understand why you feel the way you do. One of these might be Cognitive Behavioural Therapy (CBT). They will help you to manage your feelings and manage your anxiety. Many people find great success in speaking to a counsellor, so if you get the opportunity, then it is worthwhile.

**Mental Health Charities**: Thankfully, nowadays, there are lots of mental health charities available to young people. These charities will provide you with support and advice, and they specialise in mental health and anxiety.

**If you live in the U.K., then you could contact:**

YoungMinds – They are the 'U.K.'s leading charity fighting for children and young people's mental health.'

Their website states: "If you are a young person in need of support:

**Text the YoungMinds Crisis Messenger for free 24/7 support across the U.K. if you are experiencing a mental health crisis. If you need urgent help, text Y.M. to 85258.**

All texts are answered by trained volunteers, with support from experienced clinical supervisors. Texts are free from E.E., O2, Vodafone, 3, Virgin Mobile, B.T. Mobile, GiffGaff, Tesco Mobile and Telecom Plus."

**If you live in the U.S., then you could contact:**

NAMI (National Alliance on Mental Illness) – They are the U.S.'s "largest grassroots mental health organisation dedicated to building better lives for the millions of Americans affected by mental illness."

Their website states that:

**"To contact the NAMI HelpLine, please call 800-950-NAMI (6264), Monday through Friday from 10 a.m. to**

**6 p.m., E.T., or send an email to <u>info@nami.org</u>. If you need immediate help, then you could ring 911 or contact the: Crisis Text Line – Text NAMI to 741-741 to connect with a trained crisis counselor to receive free, 24/7 crisis support via text message."**

If you live anywhere else in the world, please Google "Young People's Mental Health Charities" or something similar. Remember, if you need help, help is out there.

**Notes:**

..................................................................

..................................................................

..................................................................

..................................................................

..................................................................

..................................................................

..................................................................

..................................................................

..................................................................

..................................................................

# P

## IS FOR

## PANIC

# P is for Panic

## What is panic?

Panic is a strong and sudden feeling of fear that stops you from experiencing rational and reasonable actions and thoughts.

## What is a panic attack?

A panic attack is a type of fear response. It is an overwhelming increase of thoughts and feelings, above and beyond your body's usual response to stressful, dangerous, or exciting situations.

So, basically, panic and panic attacks don't sound too great, do they?

If you have ever experienced panic or a panic attack, you will know that it is not a nice feeling.

## What does a panic attack feel like?

- You might feel your heartbeat faster.
- You might hyperventilate (struggle breathing).
- You might feel dizzy or lightheaded.
- You might feel sick.

- You might feel like you are going to have a heart attack.
- You might feel like you are going to die.
- You might feel disconnected from your body.
- Or you might experience lots of other horrible thoughts, feelings, and symptoms.

It is worth noting that if your symptoms are due to a panic attack, you will not have a heart attack, and you will not die - as much as it may feel like it at the time. It is also worth remembering – **PANIC ATTACKS WILL ALWAYS END**.

## How long does a panic attack last?

A panic attack lasts typically from between 5-30 minutes, although some can last longer. They usually peak around 10 minutes in and then settle down after 20 minutes. However, the feelings of anxiety can last for much longer afterwards. It is also possible to have more than one panic attack in a short space of time. However, with the right skills and knowledge, you should be able to help yourself.

## When could a panic attack happen?

Panic attacks can happen at any time, anywhere, anyplace. However, for some people, it may be triggered by certain situations, places, or people. For example, someone who is scared of flying may only experience panic attacks at the airport. Or someone who has social anxiety because of bullying may experience panic attacks on a Sunday night before going back to school. Panic attacks can affect everyone differently. Some people will never experience them, some people might only ever experience one, and some might experience them daily. However it affects you; short term and longer-term help are always at hand.

## So, how can you help to prevent panic attacks?

**Talk** - Once again, talk about how you are feeling to someone you trust. Building up fear and worry without talking to someone is not good for you and can result in panic.

**Breathe** - Practice regular breathing exercises like the ones in this book.

**Exercise** - Exercise regularly to allow your body to use up its flight or fight adrenaline stores and release your endorphins.

**Avoid** - Avoid stimulants like caffeine, alcohol, and drugs.

**Eat** - Eat regular meals so that your blood sugar levels remain stabilised and do not fluctuate.

**Relax** - Find moments in your day to allow your mind and body to relax – see the relaxation section of this book.

**Learn** - Learn to manage your anxiety. In managing your anxiety better, you will be less likely to experience panic attacks.

## What to do if you have a panic attack?

**Deep Breathing** – When we experience a panic attack, we can suffer from hyperventilation. Therefore, we need to try and regain control of our breathing. Please check the Breathing section for deep breathing techniques.

**Do Not Fight Your Panic Attack** – As this may make you feel worse. Instead, try to control it through breathing and distraction/grounding techniques.

**Remember That It Is A Panic Attack** - Remind yourself that you will not die, and it will pass.

**Try A Grounding Or Distraction Technique** - Like the ones mentioned in this book. The 54321 method or the Alphabet Game work well.

**Close Your Eyes** - If everything is overwhelming you, you can always close your eyes when deep breathing and thinking about your grounding techniques.

# IS FOR QUOTES

# &

# AFFIRMATIONS

# Q is for Quotes &

# Affirmations

**In this chapter, we will look at some quotes that can relate to worry and anxiety. These are by famous or inspirational people from history.**

"The person who removes a mountain begins by carrying away small stones."

Chinese Proverb

"To keep the body in good health is a duty...otherwise, we shall not be able to keep our mind strong and clear."

Buddha

"If you want to be happy, be."

Leo Tolstoy

"The beginning is perhaps more difficult than anything else, but keep heart, it will turn out all right."

Vincent Van Gogh

"Those who mind don't matter, and those who matter don't mind."

Unknown

"Life is a balance of holding on and letting go."

Rumi

"For every minute you are angry, you lose 60 seconds of happiness."

Ralph Waldo Emerson

"If you fell down yesterday, stand up today."

H. G. Wells

"Nothing in life is to be feared. It is only to be understood."

Marie Curie

"Happiness depends upon ourselves."

Aristotle

"Never stop being a good person because of bad people."

Unknown

"You yourself, as much as anybody in the entire universe, deserve your love and affection."

Buddha

"This, too, shall pass."

Persian Proverb

## What are Affirmations?

Affirmations are positive statements that you can say out loud or in your head. They can help you to overcome any negative feelings you have about yourself or your anxieties.

It is believed that by repeating them often, you will believe them, and positive changes may happen in your life.

Examples of affirmations include:

I AM HAPPY

I LOVE MYSELF

I CAN CONTROL MY ANXIETY

GOOD THINGS HAPPEN TO ME

I AM CONFIDENT

I BELIEVE IN MYSELF

Try writing down some affirmations relatable to your life and practice saying them regularly:

………………………………………………………………...

………………………………………………………………...

………………………………………………………………...

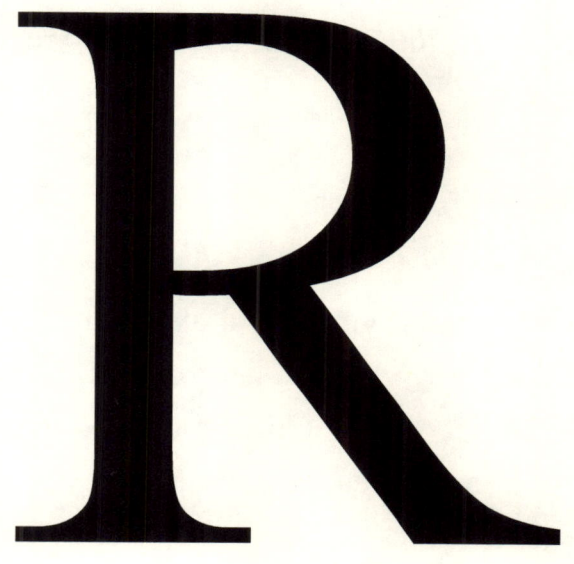

# IS FOR

# RELAXATION

# R is for Relaxation

If you suffer from anxiety (or even if you do not), it is important to find times in your day and life to enjoy some relaxation.

## What is relaxation?

Relaxation is basically the opposite of stress and anxiety. It is a state in which your mind and body feel calm and relaxed. I am sure you have felt relaxed at one point or another. Whether that is chilling out in your room, on holiday by the pool, reading a book, playing a game or something else.

Some people find it easy to relax, whereas some people find it more difficult. What is important, though, is to find time times in our day and week where we can dedicate it to relaxing - your chill time. So, what can you do to relax:

**Deep Breathing** – Try one of the many strategies written in this book.

**Reading** – Read your favourite book or magazines.

**Go For A Walk In Nature** – Go for a walk with friends or family and take your dog if you have one.

**Hobbies** – Do you have a hobby that you find relaxing? If so, great! If not, maybe think about taking one up.

**Drawing Or painting** – This can be therapeutic, and there are lots of colouring books and apps out there for all abilities.

**Listening To Relaxing Music** – Unwind by putting your feet up and listening to your favourite music.

**Just Sit In Silence** – Just take a few minutes to sit quietly in silence and enjoy the peace and quiet.

**Feeding The Birds** – Do you have a local park? If so, go with your friends or family and feed the birds. Nature and doing good deeds go well together.

**Play With Your Pet** – If you have a pet, spend some time with them. Playing with our pets can really boost our serotonin levels which is the body's happy hormone.

Try and find at least 20-30 minutes a day to relax or do something relaxing. An example might be that on Monday after school you are going to listen to relaxing music for 30 minutes before you do your homework.

Complete the following and use it as your relaxation plan.

**Monday**: What are you going to do to relax, how long for and when will you do it?

..................................................................

..................................................................

..................................................................

**Tuesday**: What are you going to do to relax, when will you do it and how long for?

..................................................................

..................................................................

..................................................................

**Wednesday**: What are you going to do to relax, when will you do it and how long for?

..................................................................

..................................................................

..................................................................

**Thursday**: What are you going to do to relax, when will you do it and how long for?

..................................................................

...................................................................

...................................................................

**Friday**: What are you going to do to relax, when will you do it and how long for?

...................................................................

...................................................................

...................................................................

**Saturday**: What are you going to do to relax, when will you do it and how long for?

...................................................................

...................................................................

...................................................................

...................................................................

**Sunday**: What are you going to do to relax, when will you do it and how long for?

...................................................................

...................................................................

...................................................................

# IS FOR SOCIAL
# MEDIA

# S is for Social Media

Now, I am sure you know what social media is. But just in case you do not, they are web-based applications where you can share information with your friends, family, and other people.

But let's face it, you are a social media generation. It is everywhere, and almost every teenager uses it. You could teach me a thing or two about it, I am sure. From TikTok to YouTube, to Instagram to Facebook. From Reddit, Twitch, Twitter, Snapchat and the many other platforms and apps that are out there. Social media is everywhere, and it is not going anywhere.

## Social media can be amazing as it can:

- Connect you with friends.
- Connect you with family.
- Be educational.
- Inform you of current events in the world.
- Introduce you to new experiences.
- Introduce you to new ideas.
- Help people to build businesses.
- Help people to grow ideas.

- Help people to showcase skills and talents.
- And so much more…

However, there is also a darker side to social media. Overusing social media can lead to feelings of anxiety and poor mental health. Let's have a look at why…

## The negatives of social media:

**Usage** - You might use it too much that it affects your life. It might stop you from seeing friends and family and getting out and about and being active.

**Sleep** - It can affect your sleep and cause sleep deprivation if you use it or check it late at night.

**Cyberbullying** - You might experience cyberbullying. This is a form of bullying that takes place online.

**Compare** - You might compare your life to other peoples and feel inadequate as a result.

**Peer Pressure** - You might experience peer pressure. This is where people put you under pressure to do something you do not want to do.

**Pressure** - You might feel pressure to respond quickly to messages.

**Worry** - You might worry about what people think about your posts or pictures.

Here are some statistics to show you the impact social media can have on young people:

- A recent report in the USA suggested that over 50% of U.S. teens experienced online harassment or cyberbullying. Furthermore, 9 in 10 thought that this was something that affected their peers and 6 in 10 believed that it is a huge problem.
- The same report also suggested that 1 in 4 young people believe that social media has a mostly negative effect.
- There are also countless studies that have linked social media use in young people with poor sleep and mental health problems such as anxiety.

So, what can you do to make sure you are getting the best out of social media and not the worst?

## Social Media Top Tips

**Do Not Spend Too Much Time On There** – Be mindful of how long you are on there. Try and limit yourself to under 1 hour a day. There should be a section on your phone where you can monitor your daily usage.

**Do Not Spend Too Much Time On It Late At Night** – Try not to be on your phone before you go to sleep and try not to check it in the night.

**Be Careful What You Share On Social Media** – Do not share anything you wouldn't want strangers to see.

**Be Careful Who You Speak To** – Only speak to your family and friends on there. If strangers contact you, ignore them, block them, and speak to a trusted adult about it.

**Do Not Compare Yourself To Other People** – You may see people post pictures or videos that make you wish you had their life. This is called FOMO or Fear of Missing Out. Remember, everyone is different, and not everything you see is real (see below). Focus on your life and the good things in it.

**Understand That Not Everything You See Is Real** – An image or video on social media does not always tell the true story. Many of them are posed, filtered, photoshopped or not a true reflection of someone's life. Likewise, there may be content that people share that is 'Fake News' or 'Deep Fake'. This is content that is not actually real and has been made to manipulate people.

**Follow Only Positive Pages And Influencers** – Make sure to only follow pages and influencers promoting positive messages. Also, remember to be a positive influence on others with what you post.

**Make Sure To Maximise Real Life Contact With Family And Friends** – Social media is no replacement for real-life contact. Make sure to get lots of face-to-face time in with your loved ones.

**Notes:**

...............................................................................

...............................................................................

...............................................................................

...............................................................................

...............................................................................

...............................................................................

...............................................................................

...............................................................................

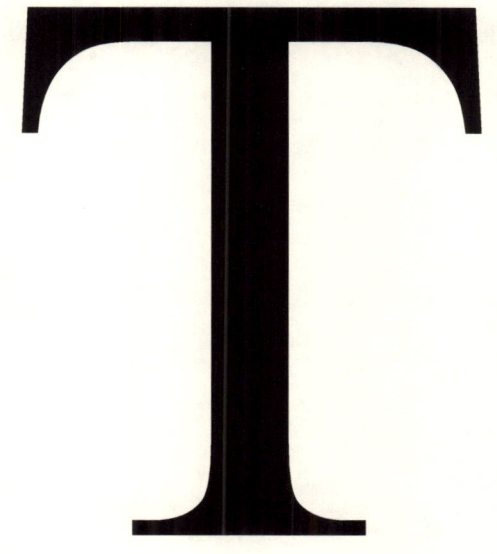

# IS FOR TAKING

# CONTROL

# T is for Taking Control

In this section of the book, we will look at some more tips to help you regain control over your anxiety. Along with the tips and strategies already mentioned in this book, these should help you to manage your anxious feelings going forward.

## Do Not Be Scared Of Anxiety

Firstly, and importantly – do not be scared of anxiety. As scary as it can be, the trick is not to be scared by it. Understand that it is your body and mind reacting to your thoughts and that you can learn to control them using the techniques in this book.

## Learn What Works For You

There are lots of different tips and strategies for coping with anxiety. However, you need to find the ones that work for you. Try them all and see which works best. This is where a journal or mood tracker can help.

## Understand You Are Not Alone

It is important to realise that you are not alone with your anxiety. If you feel alone, that can be really scary. However, there is lots of help out there for you, and people to talk to. Remember, 1 in 6 young people were reported to have a mental health problem in England in 2020, so there are lots of other young people who feel just like you do.

## Understand Thoughts And Feelings Are Not Facts

Sometimes your anxious thoughts and feelings can confuse you by making you think certain things about yourself. It can also make you question what others think about you. But these thoughts and feelings are not necessarily facts. For example, you may think that you are fat when you are actually quite slim. It might make you think you are a bad person when actually you are a good person. It might make you think people hate you when actually they like you. The next time you have anxious or worrying thoughts, ask yourself – are these feelings facts or am I overthinking things?

## Stop Catastrophising

Catastrophising basically means that you think of the worst-case scenario in a situation. For example, if you have a test and you convince yourself that you will fail before even trying. This means you have let your thoughts catastrophise and have decided that the worst possible outcome will happen. Well, there is a big chance you might pass the exam, so concentrate on the positives. The next time you have anxious thoughts, ask yourself if you are catastrophising and if you should think of a more positive outcome.

## Be Around People Who Support You

Whether you are suffering from anxiety or not, it is always important to be around people who make you feel safe, happy and support you. Do not surround yourself with negative people, toxic people or those who cause you trouble.

## Be Open And Honest With Those Around You

For the people around you to support you, you need to be open and honest about how you are feeling. Do not keep your thoughts and worries bottled up. Instead, share them with people who care for you.

## Only Do As Much As You Can Do

Having anxiety can be really tough, so it's important to only do as much as you can do. If something is going to cause you severe anxiety or lead to a panic attack, then it is okay to say no to doing it. As you get better at controlling your anxiety, you may become better in certain situations. But only do as much as you can do until you feel stronger.

## Make a Plan

If you are suffering from anxiety, then you need to make a plan. Decide how you are going to control it and the things that you are going to do. Are you going to speak to certain people, start exercising, eat healthier, try breathing techniques or something else? Make a plan to help you get better and follow it through.

## Set Small Daily Goals

Having anxiety is tough. That is why it is important to set yourself small and achievable goals so you feel a sense of achievement. What those are is up to you. Some examples might be to complete all your homework on time, to tidy your room, to do some exercise, to answer a question in class or something else.

# U

## IS FOR
### UNDERSTANDING
## IT'S OKAY

# U is for Understanding It's Okay

One of THE most important things to understand and remember when you are suffering from anxiety is that:

**It's Okay Not To Be Okay!**

You may have heard of this before - and it is true.

It is okay to feel rubbish, and it is okay to feel anxious. It is okay to worry, have fears and experience panic.

It is not nice, but it is okay to feel those feelings, and they can be completely normal feelings to have. However, we do not want to experience them all the time.

The most important thing for you to realise is that you are not:

- Weird
- Attention seeking
- Alone
- Strange
- Different

- Stupid
- Going Crazy

And you should never be:

- Ashamed.
- Embarrassed.
- Scared to talk to someone about it.
- Made to feel bad about it.
- Not believed about how you are feeling.
- Left to suffer in silence.

In this section we will look at some statistics from the adult population that will show you JUST how common anxiety is.

**Statistic 1**

A leading U.K. mental health charity reported that in March 2020, around 50% of people in the U.K. reported a high rating of anxiety. This is the equivalent to more than 25 million people.

**Statistic 2**

A commonly held statistic in the U.K. is that 1 in 4 people will experience a mental health problem in any given week.

**Statistic 3**

A leading mental health charity in the U.S.A estimates that anxiety disorders affect over 40 million adults every year.

. . . . . . . . . .

Are you surprised by these statistics? You see, it is probably more common than you first thought. That is why it is important to understand:

## It's Okay Not To Be Okay!

. . . . . . . . . .

**Activity**

**Case Study 1**

Jenny is worried that she is suffering from anxiety. She thinks she is weird and different and does not want to speak to anyone about it. She has confided in you, though. What could you say to her?

...........................................................................

...........................................................................

...........................................................................

.............................................................

.............................................................

.............................................................

## Case Study 2

Freddie has panic attacks. He does not know why, but it is making him scared and upset. He feels ashamed about this and thinks that he is the only person who suffers from this. You are his best friend, so he has told you. What could you say to him?

.............................................................

.............................................................

.............................................................

.............................................................

.............................................................

.............................................................

# IS FOR VIDEO
# GAMES

# V is for Video Games

Video Games are just another name for the computer games you play on your Xbox, PlayStation, Nintendo Switch, phones, and other consoles.

They are great fun, right? We all love playing games - even Grandma's and Grandads.

They can be a great place to socialise with your friends, and they can be exciting and relaxing all at the same time. Studies have even shown that playing games can develop friendships and communication, which can help you to be less anxious.

Sounds great! Well, like social media, they can be. However, they also need limits to make sure they are used for the better and not the worst.

So, here is a list of the things to keep an eye on so they do not lead to you feeling anxious.

**Do Not Spend Too Much Time Playing Games** – Enjoy playing computer games but do not let them get in the way of real face to face time with your family and friends. Also, do not let it get in the way of your homework or other hobbies and interests you enjoy.

**Do Not Play Games Too Late At Night** – Make sure to switch off your games well before going to bed. Playing computer games too late can lead to poor sleeping habits and sleep deprivation. This can cause anxious feelings and make your anxiety worse.

**Watch Who You Speak To** – Make sure you know who you are gaming with and keep it to your friends and family. There might be strangers gaming online who say mean and bad things to you. They might also try and pressure you into doing things or request things from you. These types of people are dangerous and can make your experience more anxious.

**Do Not Get Stressed Out Playing Them** – Sometimes, the game can get the better of us, or another player might be better than us. It is important not to get stressed out about these things and just enjoy playing the game. Feelings of anger or envy can all result in feelings of anxiousness. So, remember to play games for fun.

**Do Not Spend Money You Do Not Have** – Many games require you to buy extra items on them. If this is the case, do not spend money you do not have (including your parents). This can lead to debt which can make you and your parents feel anxious.

**Watch Out For Bullying** – If the people you are playing with call you names or are mean to you, do not accept it. Make sure not to play with them again unless they can learn to be kinder. Bullying can make you feel sad and anxious, so make sure to watch out for it. Speak to an adult if you think it is happening. Also, on the other hand, do not be a bully.

**Notes:**

..................................................................

..................................................................

..................................................................

..................................................................

..................................................................

..................................................................

..................................................................

..................................................................

..................................................................

# IS FOR WORRY

# W is for Worry

**What is worry?**

To worry is to think about things or problems that could happen, in a way that results in you feeling sad, scared or unhappy.

I am sure you have experienced worry before – it's not nice, is it - however, it is normal to worry about things. You might worry about an exam, your doctor's appointment, whether you will be judged by other young people or something else.

**So, what is the difference between worry and anxiety?**

Well, to be honest, they are very similar. However, worrying tends to be more the thoughts in your head, whereas anxiety could be seen to be the feelings and the symptoms you experience because of worrying. They really do go hand in hand. Like an evil duo that needs defeating by a superhero with super wellbeing tips....you!

## How can we stop worrying?

Well, a little bit of worrying is normal and okay. It is not nice, but it's normal. However, a lot of worrying can be extremely unhealthy and can develop into an anxiety disorder.

So how can we stop worrying so much about things that are out of our control? Let's have a look at some tips to help you deal with your worries and make sure the evil duo of worry and anxiety do not beat you down:

**Worry Time** - Worry time is where you allocate a specific time in the day to worry or think about your anxieties. To use this strategy throughout the day, make a note of your worries on paper or your phone and then come back to them at a specific time later on. Do not think about them when they occur but take control over them and revisit them later. When you do revisit them, think about them mindfully and use a breathing technique, as shown in this book. Make sure that you are relaxed when you do so. There are smartphone apps that can help you with this. One worth looking at is WorryTime by reachout.com.

**Worry-Free Time -** Worry-free time, on the other hand, is a time for you to do something that you enjoy and can distract you from your worries. It should be something that takes a bit of concentration but makes you feel good or rewarded for doing it. Worry-free activities might include playing an instrument, swimming, doing puzzles, reading, painting, getting creative or something else you are interested in. Make sure to build half an hour or an hour of worry-free time into your day to give you a break from your anxious thoughts. This can involve setting your mini-goals for your day.

**Write Down Your Worries** - As mentioned above, you could write down your worries in a journal. That way, you can reflect on them either that day or another day. Sometimes, the act of writing things down can help to ease tension and stress that is building up within you.

**Speak About Your Worries** - Always speak about your worries with someone you trust. A problem shared is a problem halved, so make sure to talk about how you are feeling. Make sure you have at least one person you can talk to, but the more, the better. Remember, you are not weird or strange, and whatever you are worrying about, there will be other people who worry about similar things.

**Embrace Uncertainty** - In our lives, there are going to be lots of things we cannot control. This is just the way life is. If you can learn to understand and accept that sometimes there are things that will be out of your control, then you will be able to deal with your worries and anxieties better.

**Go Easier On Yourself** - Remember to go easy on yourself. Having anxiety and worrying can be hard work, so do not put added pressure on yourself to be perfect. Remember that it is okay to worry a little. Just put your strategies into place, and you will feel better.

**Notes:**

...........................................................

...........................................................

...........................................................

...........................................................

...........................................................

...........................................................

...........................................................

...........................................................

...........................................................

...........................................................

# IS FOR eXTRA

# TIPS

# X is for eXtra Tips

In this section, we will look at all those eXtra little tips that might help you to cope with your anxiety.

**Be Thankful** - Sometimes, when we feel anxious or worry a lot, we forget about the good things that we have in our life. That is why it is important to be thankful for the positive things that you do have. Remember to tell yourself, "I am thankful for my parents or carers", "I am thankful for my school friends", "I am thankful for having a phone and my pocket money", or whatever else you are thankful for. This can help to create a positive mindset, particularly when you are feeling down. This is also called practising gratitude.

**Keep A Tidy Bedroom** - It is important to keep a tidy bedroom as lots of clutter in your everyday space can create a chaotic mind. You should aim to keep your surroundings tidy and peaceful and make your bedroom a place of relaxation. It should not be a stressful place to be.

**Do Not Be Scared Of Anxiety** - Easier said than done, right? Well, after learning all of the techniques in this book and understanding anxiety better, you should hopefully be less scared of it. You have lots of coping strategies to deal with it, so do not be scared of it. Just use your techniques to manage it the best you can.

**Cold Water** - There are lots of benefits of water for the body. Firstly, you should always keep hydrated as suffering from dehydration can make you feel anxious. Furthermore, cold water can also help when experiencing extreme anxiety or panic. This is because our bodies can feel warm as our heart races. So, try putting cold water on your wrists and on the back of your neck to help you cool down.

**Put Your Positive Moments In A Jar** - Try writing down positives from your day and life and then putting them in a jar. Whenever you feel low or down, take your little moments out of the jar, read them, and remember the good things in your life.

**Get A Hobby** - If you have not got one already, then a hobby can really help with feelings of anxiety and stress. It can give you something positive and fun to focus your energies on. It can also feel rewarding. This could be sports, keeping fit, colouring, drawing or something else.

**Stress Balls, Fidget Spinners and Silly Putty** -These objects have all been shown to help lower feelings of anxiety. Particularly for people who fidget with their hands. It can also give your brain something to focus on doing so you are distracted from having anxious thoughts.

**Weighted Blankets** - Weighted blankets can feel really comforting, and they can help you to relax and get a good night's sleep. They have an earthing effect that makes your body feel like it is being pushed towards the ground. This deep pressure is said to relieve symptoms of anxiety while lowering your levels of cortisol (stress hormone) in your body.

**Notes:**

........................................................................

........................................................................

........................................................................

........................................................................

........................................................................

........................................................................

........................................................................

........................................................................

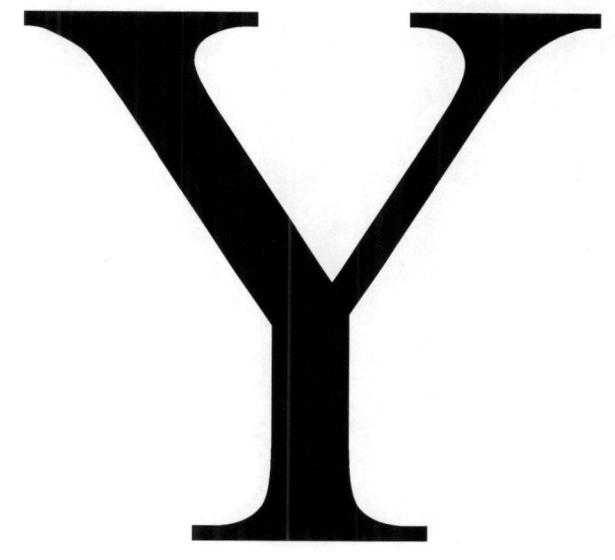

# IS FOR YOUR
# PLAN

# Y is for Your Plan

On the following pages, write down all the things that make you anxious or worried and create your action plan to take control of them.

What are you anxious about?

..................................................................

..................................................................

..................................................................

..................................................................

..................................................................

How anxious does it make you feel on a scale of 1-10?

..................................................................

..................................................................

What techniques will you use to help manage your anxiety?

..................................................................

..................................................................

...................................................................

...................................................................

...................................................................

...................................................................

Who will you speak to about your anxieties and worries?
(This is extremely important)

...................................................................

...................................................................

...................................................................

...................................................................

...................................................................

**Remember to speak about how you are feeling.**

What are you anxious about?

...................................................................

...................................................................

...................................................................

...................................................................

..................................................................

How anxious does it make you feel on a scale of 1-10?

..................................................................

..................................................................

What techniques will you use to help manage your anxiety?

..................................................................

..................................................................

..................................................................

..................................................................

..................................................................

..................................................................

Who will you speak to about your anxieties and worries? (This is extremely important)

..................................................................

..................................................................

..................................................................

..................................................................

# Z

# IS FOR ZZZ's

# (Sleeping)

# Z is for Zzz's (Sleeping)

Life can be tiring. Anxiety can be tiring. That is why it is important to try and get 8 hours of good sleep every night. The less sleep you get, the more anxious you are likely to feel. So, what can you do to help yourself get a good night's sleep, and what should you not do? Let us start with:

**Bad Sleeping Habits**

**Being On Your Phone Too Late** - As much as you enjoy being on your phone and scrolling through TikTok or any other site, being on it too late can overstimulate your mind. Screens such as phones and T.V.'s produce blue light. This is reported to stimulate the mind and suppress the 'sleep hormone melatonin. This can lead to difficulty falling asleep and bouts of insomnia (difficulty falling asleep, staying asleep or waking up often).

**Checking Your Phone In The Middle Of The Night** - Waking up and checking your phone in the middle of the night is another no-no. Checking for messages, updates or replying to people can cause your mind to become overstimulated and awake. This can cause you trouble in falling back to sleep resulting in a bad night's sleep for you.

146

**Playing Computer Games Too Late** - Similar to being on your phone too late, playing computer games too late can also overstimulate your mind. Try switching off at least an hour before bed to give yourself a better chance at relaxing.

**Napping Too Late In The Day** - A 20-minute power nap can sometimes be helpful if we are extremely tired. However, napping too late in the day can create trouble when trying to fall asleep at night. To avoid this, do not nap after 2 pm in the day.

**Avoid The News Before Bed** - The news can be stressful and worrying, so avoid reading or watching it before you go to bed.

**Avoid Stimulants Like Caffeine** - Tea, coffee, dark chocolate and energy drinks all have caffeine in them. If you want to sleep well, avoid these before bed.

## Good Sleeping Habits

**Read A book** - Reading can be extremely relaxing, with studies showing that it can help to reduce stress by over 60%. Pick your favourite book or magazine and try reading to relax before bed.

**Try Deep Breathing**– Please see the Breathing section in this book.

# Conclusion

If you have made it to the end of this book, congratulations. Go you!

I hope you now understand more about anxiety than you did before and that you have learned lots of new strategies and tips to help you cope with any anxious feelings.

You can use this book as your little friend as and when you need it.

Remember to talk to people about how you are feeling and to look after your wellbeing. Speak to your friends and family and be supportive of your friends who might be struggling also.

If you need more help, then check out the OTHER SUPPORT section.

Good luck and keep healthy.

Manufactured by Amazon.ca
Bolton, ON

24296275R00090